Cambridge English Readers

Starter Level

Series editor: Philip Prowse

Dirty Money

Sue Leather

D0569939

CAMBRIDGE
UNIVERSITY PRESS

CAMBRIDGE UNIVERSITY PRESS
Cambridge, New York, Melbourne, Madrid, Cape Town, Singapore, São Paulo

Cambridge University Press
The Edinburgh Building, Cambridge CB2 2RU, UK

www.cambridge.org
Information on this title: www.cambridge.org/9780521683333

© Cambridge University Press 2006

This publication is in copyright. Subject to statutory exception
and to the provisions of relevant collective licensing agreements,
no reproduction of any part may take place without the written
permission of Cambridge University Press.

First published 2006
Reprinted 2006

Sue Leather has asserted her right to be identified as the Author of the Work in
accordance with the Copyright, Design and Patents Act 1988.

Printed in India by Thomson Press

Illustrations by Debbie Hinks

A catalogue record for this publication is available from the British Library

ISBN-13 978-0-521-68333-3 paperback
ISBN-10 0-521-68333-5 paperback

ISBN-13 978-0-521-68334-0 paperback plus audio CD pack
ISBN-10 0-521-68334-3 paperback plus audio CD pack

No character in this work is based on any person living or dead.
Any resemblance to an actual person or situation is purely accidental.

Contents

People in the story

 **Joe** works for the *Murray Echo*, a newspaper

 **Sandy** is Joe's wife

 **Dan** is Joe and Sandy's neighbour

 **Karl Johnson** is the boss of Pan Global

 **Cameron Grady** is Joe's boss

 **Ed Bains** is the boss of the *Murray Daily*

 **Ken Reid** is the mayor of Murray

Places in the story

Chapter 1 *A noise*

'Canada is beautiful,' thinks Joe. He's looking out of the window of his house. He can see water and mountains. On the water he can see a little white boat. In the big blue sky he can see an eagle. He can hear … nothing.

Joe thinks about England. It's small and dirty, he thinks. And the noise! Joe smiles. He sits and looks at the beautiful water and mountains.

'Happy, love?'

Joe's wife, Sandy, comes in with a cup of tea.

'Mmm,' says Joe, 'very happy.' He takes the tea and he drinks.

Sandy sits down too and they talk about their beautiful house. They're far from England and far from the city. Here in the little town of Murray there's no dirt and no noise. Canada is a new start for Joe and Sandy. They have new jobs too. Joe works for a newspaper, the *Murray Echo*. Sandy works at the hospital; she's a doctor.

'Tomorrow,' says Joe, 'we can have lunch by the water.'

'Mmm.' Sandy smiles.

Joe looks at Sandy and smiles too. 'Thank you for the tea,' he says.

Then Joe hears a noise.

'What's that?' he asks.

'What?' Sandy asks.

'Listen,' Joe says.

Sandy listens.

Drrrr! Drrrr!

'Is it Dan? Is he working on his house?' asks Sandy. Dan lives in the next house.

'No, that isn't Dan,' says Joe. He walks over to the window. He sees nothing. Just the mountains and the flat blue water. But he can hear the noise. A new noise.

Drrrr! Drrrr!

Joe looks up. He looks around. He looks up again. Then he sees it. On the mountain near his house he sees a big machine. It's making a noise: Drrrr! Drrrr! The machine is taking trees down. Behind it there's another big machine. It's digging a hole in the ground.

'Look at this!' Joe says to Sandy.

'What?' asks Sandy.

Near the machines is a big white sign. On the sign it says PAN GLOBAL.

'What is it?' asks Sandy.

'I don't know, but I'm going to look,' says Joe. He opens the door and runs to the mountain.

Joe stands in front of one of the big machines. The driver sees him and stops.

'What do you want?' the driver asks.

'What's this? asks Joe. He looks at the big hole in the ground. 'What's Pan Global?'

The man smiles. 'It's a mine,' he says. 'There are diamonds under here!'

Chapter 2 *Help!*

Joe goes back to his house and tells Sandy about the mine.

Ten minutes later there's someone at the door. It's Dan, Joe and Sandy's neighbour.

'Joe,' asks Dan, 'what's that noise?'

'It's a mine,' Joe says. 'We must tell everyone. This is a very bad thing.'

'The noise! The dirt!' says Dan. 'You must write about it in the newspaper.'

There's another neighbour at Joe and Sandy's door. It's Gloria Makeba. 'This noise!' she says. 'You write for the newspaper,' she says to Joe. 'You must help us!'

Joe hears the phone. It's another neighbour. 'And what about all the birds? They're going to leave!' Then another. 'The noise!' And another. 'What about the beautiful trees? They're taking down all the trees!'

All the neighbours are very angry. They all say the same thing to Joe: 'Help!'

Chapter 3 *Monday*

It's Monday and Joe is at work at the *Murray Echo*. He's writing about the mine. He looks on the internet and reads about Pan Global. There's a photo of Karl Johnson, the boss.

Joe phones Karl Johnson.

'Mr Johnson,' says Joe, 'my name is Joe Brennan and I work for the *Murray Echo*. I want to talk to you about the mine ...'

'What do you want to know?' asks Karl Johnson.

'Why are you mining near houses and people?' asks Joe.

'Because there are diamonds there!' Johnson says. 'We can sell them in Canada, in the US, in Europe. We can sell them all over the world. They're very expensive! And lots of people in Murray can work at the mine!'

Joe puts the phone down and starts to write.

'What do we know about Pan Global,' he writes, 'and why can they start mining near our houses?'

'What are you writing?'

Joe looks up. It's Cameron Grady, Joe's boss.

'I'm writing about the mine …' Joe says.

'The mine?' says Grady.

'Yes, the mine,' says Joe. 'Pan Global say there are diamonds there.'

'Mmm, really?' says Grady. 'But you must write about the tennis tournament. It's big news in Murray.'

'But what about the mine?' asks Joe.

'Well, it's important,' says Grady, 'but right now the tennis is more important.'

'But everybody in the town is angry,' says Joe. '*Everybody* wants to read about the mine!'

Grady smiles. 'Listen, Joe,' he says. 'It's just a mine. There are a lot of mines in Canada. The tennis is more important.'

Grady gives Joe a piece of paper. On the paper it says, 'Today in Murray: tennis tournament starts!'

Chapter 4 *Night drive*

Beep! Beep! Beep!

Joe looks at the alarm clock. It's three o'clock in the morning.

'What is it?' asks Sandy. 'It's only three o'clock!'

'I'm going to have a good look at the mine!' Joe says.

'Why now?' says Sandy. She closes her eyes.

Joe puts on his clothes. 'There's something wrong about all this,' thinks Joe. 'Grady wants me to write about tennis, but everyone is angry about the mine. What's going on?'

Joe leaves his house. Now there are no trees around the mine. There is a long road, made of dirt. He gets into his car and drives up the road.

Joe comes to a big sign: PAN GLOBAL MINE: DANGER. He stops his car next to the sign and gets out. Near the sign he sees the hole in the ground. It's very big now. Then Joe sees some lights behind him. It's a white car. He sees 'Security' on the car. The car is coming towards Joe.

The man in the Security car shouts at Joe: 'Hey! What are you doing?'

Joe gets back into his car and drives fast. He doesn't want to talk to the Security man. He wants to get to his house.

Joe looks in his mirror; the white car is right behind him. The white car is going very fast.

Crash! The white car drives into the back of Joe's car. Joe goes off the road and into the trees.

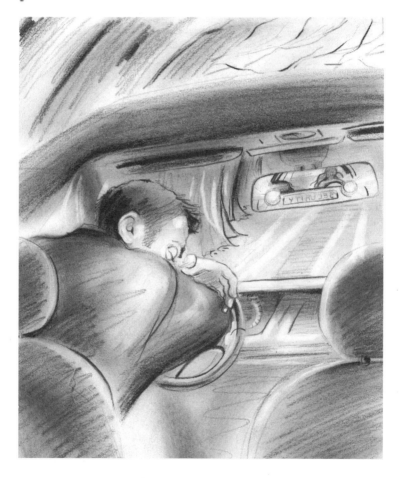

Chapter 5 *In the hospital*

Joe opens his eyes. He sees Sandy.

'Oh, Joe,' she says. 'You're all right!'

Joe looks around. He's in the hospital.

'I must get up,' says Joe. 'I must talk to Grady.'

'But ...' Sandy watches Joe. He gets out of bed.

'I must write about this mine,' says Joe.

'Not now, Joe,' says Sandy. 'You ...'

'Something is going on here,' says Joe. 'It's important.'

'Well, all right,' says Sandy. 'But wait. I can take you to work.'

Fifteen minutes later Joe is at work. 'I can't write about tennis,' he says to Grady. He tells his boss about the white car.

'And the Security man ...' Joe says.

'Forget it,' says Grady. 'You can't write about the mine. Lots of people from Murray can work there. It's a good thing!'

'But something is wrong,' says Joe. 'People are angry!'

Now Grady is getting angry.

'Listen,' says Grady. 'I'm the boss here and I'm telling you: don't write about the mine!'

Chapter 6 *The mine again*

That night Joe talks to his wife.

'Sandy, something bad is going on,' he says, 'and I think Grady knows about it.'

Sandy is afraid, but she knows her husband. She knows she can't stop him.

Joe puts on some black clothes and takes some rope and his torch. This time he walks to the mine. He looks around, but he can't see the Security man.

Joe feels afraid, but he takes the rope and ties it to a machine. Then he goes down the rope and into the hole. He turns on the torch. He can see nothing. He walks for a minute, two minutes. Now he is very afraid. He thinks about his nice warm bed. He feels very tired.

Then he sees something. It's a big white door. On the door it says: DANGER: NUCLEAR MATERIAL. AUTHORIZED PERSONNEL ONLY.

Chapter 7 *Just a job*

'No! It's a nuclear dump! They're putting old nuclear material in the mine!' Joe turns round and runs back. He goes up the rope and runs down the long road. He looks for the Security car, but he can't see it.

'The water!' thinks Joe. 'The trees, the birds ... the people!'

Joe runs and runs, back to his house. He's very tired. Sandy is happy to see her husband again.

'It's not diamonds! They're putting nuclear material in the mine!' he says to Sandy. 'It's a nuclear dump!'

'What!' says Sandy. 'We're living next to a nuclear dump?!'

'Who knows about this?' asks Joe. 'Somebody knows . . .'

Joe and Sandy talk for a long time. In the morning, Joe knows what he has to do. 'There's another newspaper in Murray!' he thinks.

At nine o'clock the next morning Joe goes to see Ed Bains at the *Murray Daily*.

'Mmm,' says Ed Bains, 'it's a good story. And somebody knows about it. Can you find out who?'

'I'm going to try,' says Joe. 'Then can I write the story in the *Murray Daily*?'

'Yes,' says Ed, 'but Grady isn't going to like it. What about your job at the *Murray Echo*?'

'It's just a job,' Joe says. 'This is important.'

Chapter 8 *Grady*

Wednesday evening, Thursday evening, Friday evening, Saturday evening. Every evening Joe sits in Sandy's car across the street from Cameron Grady's house. He wears a baseball cap and a false moustache.

'Grady knows something,' thinks Joe.

At work Joe doesn't say anything to Grady. He just writes about the tennis tournament.

Sunday comes. Joe is across the street from Grady's house. At nine o'clock, Grady leaves his house and he gets into his car. Joe drives behind Grady's car through the streets of Murray.

Grady drives to a bar called Milligans. He goes into the bar and Joe goes in too. Joe gets a drink and stands far away from Grady. There are a lot of people in the bar. Grady meets two men. Joe looks over at the men. One of them is Karl Johnson, the boss of Pan Global, but who is the other? He's short with black hair and a fat, round face. Joe looks and looks. Can it be ...? It's the boss of the town of Murray – it's the mayor! It's Ken Reid! The mayor of Murray!

Chapter 9 *Dirty money*

The three men are laughing and drinking; they're good friends. Joe finishes his drink and leaves the bar. Then he waits in his car across the street. Thirty minutes, an hour, two hours. Everybody leaves the bar, but the three men do not.

At 11.30, Grady, Johnson and Reid leave the bar. It's very dark and there's no-one in the street. Joe watches.

The three men stand in the street. Johnson takes something out of his pocket. Joe sees two brown envelopes. Johnson gives one envelope to the mayor and one envelope to Grady. Johnson walks away to his car.

Joe takes out his mobile phone and he phones 9-1-1. The police.

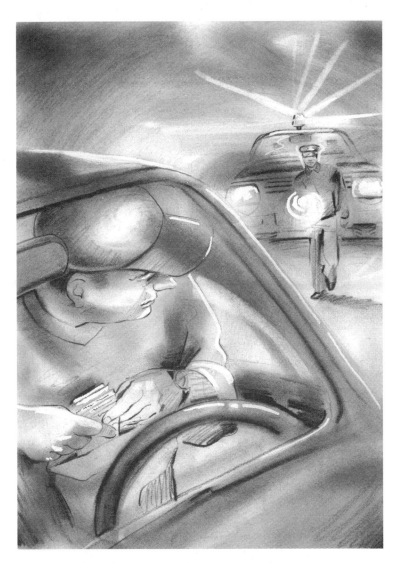

Joe watches the mayor. The mayor can't wait. He goes to his car, opens the envelope and takes some money out of it. He starts counting the money. He's nearly finished when the police get there.

Chapter 10   *A new job*

'Mayor and newspaper boss get $500,000 and Murray gets a nuclear dump!' writes Joe.

Joe is sitting at home and he's writing his story. The mayor, Grady and Johnson are with the police.

Joe finishes the story and e-mails it to Ed Bains at the *Murray Daily.*

Soon Ed is on the phone.

'Hey, Joe,' he says, 'this is a great story. Why don't you come and work for me?'

Joe says yes. He puts the phone down. He looks at the beautiful mountains and the water and listens. He can hear … nothing.

Cambridge English Readers

Look out for these other titles at the new Starter level:

The Penang File
by Richard MacAndrew
The English Prince is in Penang, Malaysia. But
so is Sergio, and Sergio wants to kill him. Can
Ian Munro find Sergio before it is too late?

ISBN-13 978-0-521-68331-9 paperback
ISBN-10 0-521-68331-9 paperback
ISBN-13 978-0-521-68332-6 paperback plus audio CD
ISBN-10 0-521-68332-7 paperback plus audio CD

What a Lottery!
by Colin Campbell
Rick loves music and wants to be a rock star.
But he has no money and his wife leaves him.
Then he wins the lottery. Is this the start of a
new life for Rick?

ISBN-13 978-0-521-68327-2 paperback
ISBN-10 0-521-68327-0 paperback
ISBN-13 978-0-521-68328-9 paperback plus audio CD
ISBN-10 0-521-68328-9 paperback plus audio CD

Let Me Out!
by Antoinette Moses
John makes a robot and calls him Nolan. Nolan can
do anything John wants. But Nolan isn't happy …

ISBN-13 978-0-521-68329-6 paperback
ISBN-10 0-521-68329-7 paperback
ISBN-13 978-0-521-68330-2 paperback plus audio CD
ISBN-10 0-521-68330-0 paperback plus audio CD

www.cambridge.org/elt/readers